The life-sized effigy of the Black Prince fully armed is made of copper. His head rests on his helmet, with a little dog at his feet. The marble tomb chest is surrounded by twelve enamelled shields, engraved with his arms for war and peace, with the two mottoes *Houmont* and *Ich diene*.

THE BLACK PRINCE

Replicas of the prince's achievements – surcoat, shield, helm (surmounted by a crest of a lion), gauntlets and scabbard – hang above his tomb; the originals are displayed in the south-east transept.

The wooden tester (canopy) above the effigy (see overleaf) is painted on the underside with a Throne of Mercy Trinity, surrounded by the four evangelists.

ONE OF THE LEGENDARY FIGURES of English history, the Black Prince, the eldest son of King Edward III, achieved his greatest triumph at the battle of Poitiers during the Hundred Years War between England and France in September 1356. He sealed his victory by capturing King John II. The chronicler Froissart reports that both men, captor and captive, stopped at Canterbury on their way from the Continent to London, to make offerings at the shrine of St Thomas Becket. The Black Prince had, seemingly from childhood, a special devotion to Canterbury Cathedral, to which he gave generously throughout his lifetime, and in which, according to his own wish, he was buried after a splendid funeral in a magnificent tomb. His tomb, beside the

former shrine of St Thomas Becket in the Trinity Chapel, is remarkable not only for its effigy and painting but also for the prince's armour, or 'achievements', hung above it.

At the height of the battle of Crécy in August 1346, King Edward III (r.1327–1377) received an urgent request for help from his eldest son, Edward. The king's response to the messenger, as reported by the contemporary commentator Jean Froissart (*c.*1337–*c.*1405), has become part of English folklore:

> *Sir Thomas, go back to him and to those who have sent you and tell them not to send for me again today, as long as my son is alive. Give them my command to let the boy win his spurs, for if God has so ordained it, I wish the day to be his and the honour go to him and those in whose charge I have placed him.*

The king did send reinforcements, but in the event they were not required. The English divisions, composed of archers and dismounted men-at-arms, held firm and the French fell back in defeat. The young prince had more than fulfilled his father's hopes and was well on the way to becoming a legend in his own lifetime. One of his many admirers wrote of him at Crécy:

> *He showed his valour to the French, piercing horses, laying low the riders, shattering helmets and breaking spears, skilfully parrying blows aimed against him, helping to their feet friends who had fallen, and showing to all an example in well doing.*

The prince was born at Woodstock in Oxfordshire, a favourite hunting lodge of the Plantagenets, in June 1330, and bought up at the royal court, where his environment and education were geared to the practice of war. From the beginning, as a sixteen-year-old at Crécy, the prince excelled as a warrior, and for the next twenty years he dominated warfare in Western Europe, coming to personify that combination of courage and courtesy, honour and magnanimity, that we understand today as chivalry. Although, just as the reality of fighting in the fourteenth century exhibited few signs of such gentle qualities, the prince was not in every way an attractive personality.

The Black Prince was a man of war and little else. He could be cruel, was extremely arrogant, and was largely

A portrait-effigy of the prince's mother, Philippa of Hainault (1314–1369), lies atop her tomb in Westminster Abbey. The remarkable degree of harmony that existed in the royal family is often attributed in part to Philippa's calming influence. Her most famous action was to dissuade Edward III from executing the Calais burghers after his capture of the port in 1347. She died from the plague in 1369.

The tomb of King Edward III lies beside that of his queen in Westminster Abbey. The effigy is thought to be modelled on a cast taken after his death. Twelve of the king's fourteen children were once depicted on the sides of his tomb – the Black Prince is among the six that remain.

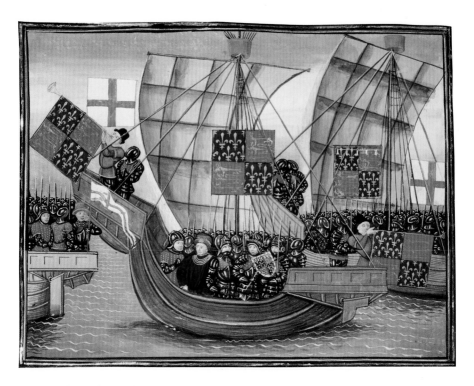

irresponsible in financial matters. Money did not trickle through his fingers so much as pour through them. Huge banquets, lavish tournaments, a vast retinue of knights and the best clothes and jewellery, in addition to an equally extravagant wife – Joan, Countess of Kent (1328–1385) – placed an intolerable burden on his resources. The need to wring every last penny from his estates led to serious disorders in Cheshire and Wales. He lacked his father's political astuteness, had little time for business, and was a poor diplomat. Brute force was usually his answer to any problem. His death at the age of 46 in 1376 was seen by many contemporaries as a disaster for England; but, in view of the considerable difficulties facing the kingdom at that time, rule by 'Edward IV' might well have been neither glorious nor successful.

A mood of euphoria swept through England following Edward III's triumph at Crécy. One contemporary was moved to write: 'The people thought that a new sun was rising over England, for the abundance of peace, the plenty of possessions and the glory of victory.' The early months of

Heavily armoured English troops embarking for France early in the Hundred Years War. The English armies were made up of volunteers and levies of national militia raised in the shires by commissions of array. A large number of ships had to be raised, with the principal source being the merchant fleets of the south coast ports.

The Battle of Sluys (24 June 1340) was Edward III's first great victory over the French in the Hundred Years War. The Black Prince was only ten at the time and so too young to fight. He was rowed out to the king's flagship to say farewell to his father shortly before the fleet set sail from England. Ten years later he would fight alongside Edward III in another navel battle, this time against a Castilian fleet, off the south coast near Winchelsea.

Quant le roy dan
gleterre z ses ma
reschaulx eurent
ordonnees leurs
batailles et leurs naires
moult richement z saigent
Ilz furent tendre et traire
les voi les contremot et vin
drent au vent de quartier
sur dextre por au lanstasse
du souleil qui en venant
leur estoit ou visaige. Si
saduiserent que ce se pvoit
tropp muyre et detterent vng

vou et tournoyent tant qlz
eurent a leur voulente. Les
normans qui les voyoient
tourner se merueilloient
pourquoy ilz se saisoient z
disoient ilz resongnet et
reculent Car ilz ne sont
pas gens pour combatre a
nous. bu voyoient les nor
mans vir les lumieres q le
roy dangleterre y estoit per
sonnelesment. Si myrent
leurs vaisseaulx en bon estat
Car Ilz estoient saiges en

9

Berkhamsted Castle, Hertfordshire, was granted to the prince on his creation as Duke of Cornwall in 1337. Repairs were carried out, and Berkhamsted became one of the prince's favourite residences.

From the end of the thirteenth century, Restormel Castle in Cornwell belonged to the Duchy of Cornwall and was therefore the property of the king's eldest son.

Caen was the first major French town to fall to the English in Edward's campaign of 1346. Even greater successes followed with victory at Crécy (see opposite) and the capture of Calais. Still only sixteen, the prince was knighted by his father after landing in France and then won his spurs at Crécy.

dieu. Qui euſt peu pren
dre partie des condicions du
Roy nˀe maiſtre et partie des
ſiennes/on en euſt bien fait
vng prince parfaict/ Car
ſans mille doubte le Roy en
ſens le paſſoit de trop/et la
fin la monſtre par ſes œuures.

 Icy parle par Incident
des querres qui furent en
Angleterre ou meſme temps.

E me ſuys oublie
en parlant de ces
matieres precedĕtes
de parler du Roy
Edouard dangleterre/Car ces
trois ſeigneurs ont veſcu dug
temps grandz/Ceſt aſſauoir
nˀe Roy/et les Duc de bour
gongne/et les Roy Edouard.
Je ne vous garde point lordre
deſcrire qui ſont les hyſtours
ny nomme les annees ny
propremẽt le temps que

11

1348 witnessed a series of spectacular tournaments, in which the prince played a prominent role. In April he became the youngest member of the Garter when his father founded the famous Order at Windsor. Such celebrations came to an abrupt and premature end with the arrival of the Black Death in the summer. Even the royal family did not escape unscathed, the prince losing a sister.

Major hostilities with the French ceased, though skirmishes still occurred, particularly in the sensitive area around Calais, taken by the English in the famous siege of 1346–47. During one of these the prince had to rescue his father who, in disguise, had plunged too recklessly into the fray. The prince again fought alongside his father in spring 1350, this time at sea, against a Castilian fleet. Given charge of his ten-year-old brother, John of Gaunt (1340–1399), the prince was nevertheless to be found in the thick of the action as the two fleets clashed in the Channel. His ship was so badly damaged that he and his men had to board and overwhelm a Castilian vessel to save themselves.

Only with the arrival of the prince in Bordeaux in September 1355 did the fighting begin in earnest again.

St George's Chapel, Windsor, was the home of the Order of the Garter, the select brotherhood of twenty-six knights founded by Edward III in 1348, for the furtherance of chivalry, religion and charity.

Edward III showed a great interest in the legend of King Arthur. The Round Table at Winchester may have been constructed early in his reign and repainted under the Tudors.

A scene from *La Livre de Chasse* (The Book of Hunting) by Gaston Phoebus, Count of Foix. The prince had a passionate interest in hunting, spending large sums of money on his horses, falcons and hounds. He met Phoebus during the *chevauchée* of 1355, when they rode together. Not wishing to alienate the powerful count, he gave strict orders that his lands should remain untouched.

The legend of the Black Prince stems from his great victories at Crécy, Poitiers and Nájera, and yet the Hundred Years War was not typified by battles. It was a war of sieges. Most towns and castles in the principal theatres of the war were subjected to direct assault or a close starvation siege. The level of destruction induced several contemporaries to write fierce criticisms of the war: 'Most people go and fight for what they can get out if it, not in the least for the love of their lord, as they pretend, or for the love of God.'

Gascony, in the south-west of France, was an extremely wealthy duchy, and Edward III had no intention of losing his lands there. The lesson of the war to date was that the duchy could only withstand the French threat with help from England. That now arrived in the shape of the prince, in his first independent command, and 2,600 men. After being joined by the local nobility, the prince moved off to the south-east on the first of his great *chevauchées* (raids). The *chevauchée* was characteristic of English military strategy in the four-

teenth century. The emphasis was not so much on the defeat of the enemy, as on their complete demoralisation through destruction, with the added prospect of profit from plunder and ransoms. In the course of eight weeks the prince and his Anglo-Gascon army covered over 500 miles, rampaging through the counties of Armagnac and Toulouse, before crossing the rivers Garonne and Ariège into Languedoc. As one English writer described their progress, 'hardly a day passed without our men taking towns, fortresses by assault, plundering them and setting them on fire'. Panic swept places as far away as Avignon, the residence of the Pope at this time, but after burning the towns of Carcassonne and Narbonne, the prince turned for home. Before disbanding his men in November, he promised them another profitable campaign in the following summer. They were not to be disappointed.

King John II of France (r.1350–1364) was determined to revenge the humiliation inflicted on him at Crécy. Unfortunately, he was no military leader and showed himself

The fortified town of Carcassonne in Languedoc was burnt by the prince and his men in the *chevauchée* of 1355.

Lacking in common sense and prone to a violent temper, King John II of France was one of the least successful kings of medieval France. Many of his difficulties stemmed from his poor relations with the powerful French nobility. He preferred the company of lower-ranking men and foreigners.

King John was fascinated by the chivalrous side of medieval warfare and founded the Order of the Star in 1351. An obvious rival to the English Order of the Garter, it had 500 members. Unfortunately, the statutes stipulated that members must not retreat more than a quarter of a mile in battle, which accounted for the loss of eighty-nine knights at Mauron in 1352. The Order had not recovered when the Battle of Poiters effectively finished it off.

At the Battle of Poitiers, the French army of around 16,000 men outnumbered the 6–7,000 Anglo-Gascon troops commanded by the prince. The longbowmen put to flight the French cavalry, but they were not so effective against the first of the dismounted French divisions led by the Dauphin Charles. Both sides fought each other to a standstill. The battle was then decided by two unforeseen events. The second French division fled, and the prince decided to advance from his strong defensive position. He sent a cavalry force to skirt round the enemy and then ordered his men to attack. The remaining French division led by King John was surrounded and, after a bitter struggle, defeated.

incapable of bringing discipline or direction to the unruly French knights. Stung into action by the tales of destruction coming from Languedoc, John intended to call the prince to account in the following year. He evidently expected him to repeat his strategy of 1355 and return to Languedoc, but in the event the prince headed north, leaving a trail of destruction through Périgord, Limousin, La Marche and into Berry and the heart of France. John mustered his forces in Orléans, ready to set off in pursuit. Meanwhile the prince pressed on into the Loire valley. Recent rains had turned the river into a raging torrent, while John's men were either guarding or had destroyed all of the bridges. So the prince led his men off to the south and distant Gascony, laden with plunder, but increasingly fearful of the large French army, now descending on the Loire bridges behind them. At Poitiers John II and his men caught up and gave battle on 19 September only to be defeated by treachery, the stubborn resistance of the Anglo-Gascon troops and the tactical genius of the prince.

Froissart had no illusions about the effects of the battle at Poitiers: 'There died that day... the finest flower of French chivalry, whereby the realm of France was sorely weakened and fell into great misery and affliction.' Even worse for France, King John, despite performing prodigious feats with his battleaxe, had also been captured. The profits of war

were never far from the thoughts of the English soldiers, not least the prince himself. Now they had claimed the greatest prize of all – the King of France. The price of King John's release in the treaty of Brétigny-Calais (1360) was three million gold crowns and the creation of a greatly enlarged English Duchy of Aquitaine in the south-west.

Out of the wreckage came hope for the future of France in the shape of the young Dauphin Charles (r.1364–1380). He had already shown his mettle in combating Edward III's campaign at Rheims in 1359–60. Edward had sought to exploit John's capture by crowning himself King of France in Rheims Cathedral, the traditional coronation site, but he had been unable to breach the city's defences. The French monarchy was on the rise again.

John II of France was captured by English troops during the Battle of Poitiers in 1356. The king was held until 1360, and the terms of his release were a heavy blow to France.

In 1362 Edward III made his eldest son Prince of Aquitaine. While Edward retained ultimate sovereignty over the duchy, the prince was given far greater authority than any previous royal lieutenant. During his rule, the prince's extravagance and vanity caused problems. According to one writer, he kept local lords waiting for four or five days for an audience.

The prince provided a sumptuous feast for John II of France at Dover Castle in July 1360, on what was supposed to be the king's last night as a captive in England. John unexpectedly returned to England early in 1364, when his son, Louis of Anjou, broke the terms of the ransom agreement. He died there in April.

The fourteenth-century Pont Valentre spans the river Lot at Cahors in the south-western province of Quercy. Cahors was handed over to the English by the treaty of Brétigny-Calais. The townspeople were far from keen, protesting: 'We are not abandoning the king; he is abandoning us to foreigners!'

Rheims Cathedral was the principal object of Edward III's ill-fated campaign of 1359–60. The English failed to take the city, forcing Edward to embark on an ultimately futile *chevauchée*, first south to the borders of Burgundy and then off to the north-west and the suburbs of Paris.

Charles V, shown here entering Paris, was the architect of French recovery from the Hundred Years War, but his personal interests were more academic and cultural than military.

The Dauphin became Charles V in 1364. He was in fact no warrior king and, perhaps more important, did not aspire to be one, as his father John II had done with such disastrous consequences for France. His skills were those of the diplomat and administrator, precisely those areas the Black Prince found difficult or tedious. Their paths never crossed, though the prince did encounter on several occasions Charles V's principal military leader, Bertrand du Guesclin (1320–1380). A native of Brittany, du Guesclin lost more battles than he won, was captured five times, and yet emerged triumphant from his struggle with the prince in Spain and Aquitaine.

Spain was divided into several kingdoms in the fourteenth century. The most powerful was Castile, hitherto a faithful ally of France. Pedro the Cruel (r.1350–1369), the then

monarch, had married a French queen, but soon developed an intense dislike for her, had her imprisoned and probably murdered. Against Pedro, Charles V moved to support Pedro's half-brother, Henry of Trastámara, later Henry II (r.1369–1379), whereupon the Castilian king turned to the English. In early 1366 du Guesclin led a large army across the Pyrenees and into Castile. Pedro, powerless to stop him, fled, via Portugal, to Gascony, leaving Trastámara to take the throne. Edward III and the Black Prince were in favour of helping Pedro. Others, such as Sir John Chandos, advised against it. The prince was not to be deterred, however, and, in return for worthless promises from Pedro, he drained his own resources and more to finance the campaign. He had also to come to an agreement with the treacherous Charles the Bad, King of Navarre, again at considerable expense, to secure safe passage through the Pyrenees.

In February 1367 the prince led his army into Spain. Charles the Bad proved to be as unreliable as ever and stage-managed his own capture by du Guesclin's troops! The prince pressed on and met Trastámara and du Guesclin at Nájera in April. Longbowmen had never before been seen in Spain, and they wrought havoc among the Trastámaran forces. Du Guesclin was captured, while Trastámara fled to Avignon. The prince had fought and won a great victory, but at a terrible cost to himself financially and physically, and it was to be his last. Pedro either could not or would not pay his vast debts, while dysentery and malaria broke out amongst the Anglo-Gascon troops, and the prince himself was struck down. Broken in health, he finally led the survivors back to Bordeaux at the end of August. He may have dreamt of returning to Castile to settle accounts with Pedro, but of more immediate concern was his desperate financial position.

The Black Prince's victory at Nájera in Spain added to his already great military reputation, but it was of dubious long-term significance. Ultimately, Pedro was unable to hold on to the Castilian throne, and the prince's health and finances were exhausted by the campaign.

Heavy taxation was promptly imposed in Aquitaine, causing an outcry from the local population. Two prominent local lords went as far as appealing to the French king over the prince's right to raise taxation. Charles V saw his opportunity to assert his authority and summoned the prince to the Parliament or royal court in Paris to answer the complaints. The prince's reply, as recorded by Froissart, was firmly in character: 'Sirs, we will gladly go to Paris to our uncle, since he has sent this to us: but I assure you that we shall have our bascinets on our heads and sixty thousand men in our company.'

As Charles undoubtedly knew, the prince was desperately ill, leaving him listless and bedridden. The war duly reopened in November 1369. The prince had already released du Guesclin, financial considerations dictating that decision. As several of the prince's councillors feared, du Guesclin promptly restored Trastámara to the Castilian throne. He also took charge of the war in the south-west of France, where his forces made steady progress. The fall of Limoges in August 1370 roused the prince to one last effort. Exhausted and embittered, he was transported in a litter to the city, where his troops stormed the defences and then indulged in 'pitiful scenes... all who could be found were put to the sword, including many who were in no way to blame'. Although the sack of Limoges was justifiable by contemporary rules of war, it proved a sad finale to a glorious military career.

The prince sailed for home in January 1371, never to return to France. His eldest son, Edward, had recently died, so he was accompanied by his wife and youngest son, Richard, destined to succeed Edward III in 1377. The Black Prince died, at the age of 46, on 8 June 1376, his body bloated and distorted by disease. There was widespread mourning at his premature death, even in France. Charles V and the French nobility attended a requiem mass held for

The Black Prince had a special affection for Canterbury Cathedral, choosing the Chapel of Our Lady Undercroft in the crypt for his final resting place. His choice was not felt to be suitably prominent, and the Black Prince's tomb was placed in the Trinity Chapel (see overleaf)l in 1376.

him in Paris, while the French writers penned solemn and favourable eulogies, the equal of anything preserved this side of the Channel.

The prince was buried on 15 October 1376. Since Henry III, the Plantagenets had had their tombs at Westminster. The prince's own choice of Canterbury for his burial place reflected his special devotion to the cathedral. The details of the funeral were carefully set out in his will:

> When our body is taken through the town of Canterbury, two war-horses covered with our arms and two men armed in our arms and in our helms shall go before our body, that is, one with our whole arms, of war quartered, and the other with our arms of peace with the badge of ostrich feathers, with four banners of the same suit; each of these to carry the said banners shall have on his head a hat with our arms. He who bears the arms of war shall have an armed man by him carrying a black pennant with ostrich feathers.

The body was to be placed on a hearse between the high altar and the choir, before being interred in the Chapel of Our Lady in the Undercroft in the crypt, in a tomb whose specifications were also carefully detailed. In the event this position for the tomb was not thought to be prominent enough, and it was finally located in the Trinity Chapel, where it is to be seen today over six centuries later.

By 1363 the prince had built a double-aisled chantry chapel in Canterbury Cathedral, in preparation for his burial in the crypt. In 1895 this became the French Protestant Church.

Despite the prince's wish to be buried in the crypt, in 1376 he was laid to rest in a magnificent tomb within the arcade of the Trinity Chapel, immediately to the south of Becket's shrine (see far right).

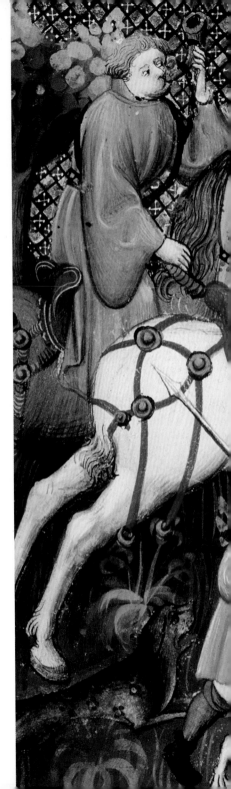

This edition © Cathedral Enterprises Ltd, 2014
Text © Cathedral Enterprises Ltd, 2014
Photography © Bridgeman Art Library, except for the
following pages: 22 © Bertl123/shutterstock.com; 14 (above)
© bonzodog/shutterstock.com; 2, 3, 30–31 © Cathedral
Enterprises Ltd; 12 (below) © Graham De'ath/
shutterstock.com; 10 (above) © donsimon/ shutterstock.com;
20–21 © Elena Elisseeva/shutterstock.com; 4–5, 28 © Robert
Greshoff/ Cathedral Enterprises; 19 (below) © Gyrohype/
shutterstock.com; 27, 29 © Angelo Hornak; 10 (below) ©
Samot/ shutterstock.com; 12 (above) © sunxuejun/
shutterstock.com; 6, 7 © Dean and Chapter of Westminster

First published in 2014 by
Scala Arts & Heritage Publishers Ltd
21 Queen Anne's Gate
London SW1H 9BU, UK
Tel: +44 (0) 20 7808 1550
www.scalapublishers.com

In association with
Cathedral Enterprises Ltd
25 Burgate
Canterbury
Kent CT1 2HA
Tel: +44 (0) 1227 865 300
www.cathedral-enterprises.co.uk
The text is a revised and updated version of an original text
first published under the same title in 1990.

ISBN: 978-1-85759-897-1

Text by David R Cook
Edited by Esme West
Designed by Nigel Soper
Printed in Turkey

10 9 8 7 6 5 4 3 2 1

FRONT COVER: Engraved portrait of the Black Prince made
after his death.

BACK COVER: Battle of Crecy, 1346, from Froissart's *Chronicle*.

INSIDE FRONT COVER: Battle of Crecy, from a fifteenth-century
manuscript.

OPPOSITE: Detail from *La Livre de Chasse* (see page 13).